THE
ILLUSION
OF CONTROL

THE ILLUSION OF CONTROL

JERRY SHULTS

Library of Congress Control Number: 2009900679
ISBN: Hardcover   978-1-4415-0635-1
                    Softcover   978-1-4415-0634-4

This book was printed in the United States of America.

To order additional copies of this book, contact:
Xlibris Corporation
1-888-795-4274
www.Xlibris.com
Orders@Xlibris.com
56955

CONTENTS

I would like to dedicate this book to my beautiful wife, Janie, and my wonderful children, Kelsey, Taylor, and Spencer. Thank you for your constant love, support, and inspiration.

I would also like to thank (my assistant) Prebah Covetz for countless hours of necessary technical and creative assistance.

And finally I would like to thank my brother and long time business partner Tom Shults for carrying a tremendous load, allowing me time to act as League City Mayor and write this book.

CHAPTER I

The Perfect Day

"The ability to concentrate and to use your time well is everything if you want to succeed in business—or almost anywhere else for that matter"~ Lee Iacocca

How long were you out of medical school before you ever really stopped to reflect on what a "perfect day" would look like? Have you even stopped to think what *any day* in the future, much less the *perfect day*, should look like? The fact is, the vision of the perfect day evolves with time. When I was a college student, the perfect day didn't even begin until noon, and it lasted until one or two a.m. Now that I am older, my perfect day ends around 11 p.m. You may be wondering what this has to do with your life and your business. Well, the answer is EVERYTHING. Regardless of what profession you are in, you need to acknowledge how you would like the day to go. By the time you begin your chosen profession, you are mature enough to realize that each day passes quickly. The days rapidly turn into weeks, months, and even years.

With the surge of cell phones, pda's, laptops, and e-mail, not to mention the time tested detractors of the telephone and junk mail; you have less free time than ever. As a medical professional, you certainly have additional distractions. These distractions may include, but are not limited to, keeping up with trade journals, continuing education, and legislative updates. This is all in addition to your office responsibilities, staff responsibilities, meetings, traveling between offices, and seeing as many patients as possible every day. Let's say for example, that you are a physician; you may see between 30-60 patients daily.

If you perform surgery or have hospital visits, the day becomes exponentially more complicated. The simple fact is, you cannot do it all, so it is imperative for you to know what is most important and what is least important. This is just as true for your personal life as it is for your professional life.

You need to decide, for example, how much time you want to dedicate towards working, exercising, and being with your family, among other things. If you do not make these decisions for yourself, someone else will make them for you, and when you start to look back over a life that has been decided by someone other than yourself, you may not like what you see. Even if you are self-employed, you may inadvertently allow someone else to decide how you spend a great deal, if not all, of your day. This may not seem like such a big deal to you; however, if you are going to allow that, please make that decision a deliberate one.

The fact is, many people need someone else to help set some parameters for their daily schedules. After all, who among us has not been thankful for a superior staff member, administrative assistant or physician's assistant, who keeps things running smoothly? Regardless of the title, these are the people who keep our days moving, and hopefully in a positive, productive direction. In addition to my staff, I rely heavily on electronic devices such as the Blackberry. Regardless of what you ultimately think about today's technology, it can make you more efficient and more productive. Therefore, when used properly, it can make your life easier.

Your staff can also track, schedule and be kept informed of your commitments with their own electronic devices. The support staff, secretaries, nurses and physician's assistants who succeed at keeping your day productive, can do so because you have established parameters for them. They excel at keeping you organized and on schedule. For example, your staff should know which days you exercise, which days you take your golf lessons, and which days you do paperwork. Your staff will also know which days you eat lunch, skip lunch, see drug reps and treat patients. The really good ones may even know which days of the year are important to remember, like your children's or spouse's birthday.

Can you imagine where you might be today, if you "*knew then what you know now*"? My guess is, when you just read that question, you probably paused briefly, and reflected over some of your early mistakes, or you just quietly laughed to yourself. This generally means you've made mistakes, like all of us, and realized many of them may have been avoidable, especially if you had a mentor. I would like to demonstrate over the next several pages what your life may look like with the addition of a business manager or mentor. Let's discover what you are doing right, what you are doing wrong, and what you are not doing at all. This is a management tool commonly known as "Start-Stop-Keep". The name is self-explanatory. What do you need to start doing, stop doing and keep doing?

Let me tell you now, what I wish I knew back then.

What I would like to accomplish is to get you to realize the direction in which you may be heading, why, and what your options may be. Many times, to understand where you are going, you must first acknowledge where you have been. The fact is, you are heading somewhere. The question is, where?

The business world and the world at large today, present many opportunities. For example, the medical field is not the same as it was twenty years ago. But what industry or profession is? Twenty years ago you would have never seen lawyers advertising on television, or the Nike swoosh on virtually every sporting uniform from Little League to the pros. This doesn't mean things are worse, just different. Together we may identify some opportunities that may be available to you, if you just take a moment to recognize how close they really are.

The most important ingredient to succeeding is to realize that you control your own destiny, whether you like it or not. And in simple, everyday terms, that means that you alone can decide how you want to manage your career. And more importantly, if you are not doing it the way you want to, there is no better time to change that than right now.

As I stated in the very beginning of this chapter, how you want to manage your career may well depend on factors such as your age, your family status, your hobbies, your lifestyle, and your retirement plans. Believe me when I say that I realize that this is only a partial list of circumstances that could affect your professional career choices.

Have you ever heard the line from the poem, "the best laid plans of mice and men oft go astray"? We all need to be prepared for circumstances beyond our control, some of which may greatly impact our professional decisions. In the late 1980's, I opened an environmental testing office for my firm in Albuquerque, New Mexico. At the time I lived in Houston. Soon I was spending three days a week in the Albuquerque office, one day a week traveling and one day a week in the Houston office. I had three children—a one year old, a two year old and a three year old. (I never did figure out what caused my children to be born only 16 months apart from each other). Six months into the new business venture, my 30 year old wife was diagnosed with breast cancer.

I immediately closed the new office, took a twelve month sabbatical and stayed home with my wife and family. There is no amount of business planning that would have prepared me for that event. You simply cannot schedule "life events" and "acts of God", but you cannot postpone your life waiting for everything to be perfect either. As it turns out, my wife is a cancer survivor and has been cancer free for almost twenty years now. And I must admit, in many ways that event had an enormous impact on my life and my goals. In so many ways, it defined who I am, and yet I had absolutely no control over it whatsoever. Although I still fall victim to working too much, like so many of us do, I also stop and realize we are all here for many reasons, work is just one of them.

Realizing what you want for yourself in your chosen profession is a mature, positive step in life. You must always remain flexible, but you must know, at least in principle, where you want to go.

Recently my wife and I were on vacation in Hawaii. We were driving around the island just taking in the beautiful scenery. Suddenly we came to a fork in the road. There was an old man selling fresh pineapple at a small stand right in the middle of the fork in the road. We decided to treat ourselves, and while enjoying our pineapple, I casually asked the man which was the best direction of the two to take. He asked me where exactly I was headed. I told him nowhere in particular, to which he quickly responded, "Then it doesn't really matter which way you go".

You can take your life and your profession virtually anywhere you want to, as long as you know where that is. To benefit from reading this book, you must ask yourself some basic questions. As you read these questions, you will realize that there are other questions that you also need to ask yourself, as well as other issues to resolve—these questions need to be answered with raw honesty. Let me caution you as you read these questions and begin to formulate answers. If you are going to write the answers down, do it on another sheet of paper that you can access without having the book with you.

This is important for a couple of reasons. First and foremost, you need to know that your answers are secure from your spouse, kids, partners, or anyone else that may pick up this book. And secondly, if you are like most professionals, you will want to reflect on this list over time.

What I mean by this is that most people have three basic personas. The first is how we see ourselves, the second is how we think the world sees us, and, of course, the third is how we actually are.

It is important to be honest with yourself while addressing these questions. Otherwise, they are meaningless. Again, these are only a few questions that you may consider.

1) Why did you originally choose your profession?
2) Why have you remained in your current field?
3) Within your profession, how much time do you spend doing what you enjoy? And by this I mean for example, if

you chose medicine because you loved healing people, how much time do you now spend healing people, as opposed to paperwork, staff meetings, etc?

4) Within your profession, why do you do things that you do not enjoy?

5) Are you satisfied with your income?

6) Are you satisfied with the number of hours you work in a week?

7) Do you have interests outside of your profession (hobbies) that you actually spend time on?

8) If so, what are they? (list in order or enjoyment and importance)

9) If not, why?

10) Do you truly plan on ever retiring?

11) When do you actually plan on retiring? (reduce this number to days, months or years)

If you can answer these questions honestly, you should be able to achieve what you always wanted to achieve from your career. Although the world of business continually changes, so do your options for dealing with that change. All we need to establish is a solid foundation. The foundation that I am referring to is simply knowing what you want for yourself. There are people who can help you identify what you want from your practice and your life; however, you have to be the one to initiate the process. It cannot, and more importantly, will not, be accomplished without your active participation.

Let's proceed in the privacy of this book to address that issue, and just hypothetically, see where that process may take us.

CHAPTER TWO

Expertise

"There is one rule of action more important than all others. It consists in never doing anything that someone else can do for you" ~ Calvin Coolidge

Three bricklayers were all working together, side by side, laying bricks. A man asked the first bricklayer, "What are you doing"? The reply came, "I am laying bricks". The man then asked the second bricklayer, "What are you doing"? The reply came," I am building a brick wall". The man then asked the third bricklayer, "What are you doing"? The reply came, "I am building a Cathedral".

The question I ask you is, "What are you doing"? Be completely honest with yourself. This is not a psychological evaluation with right or wrong answers. For instance;

1. Do you wash your own car?
2. Do you mow your own yard?
3. Do you change the oil in your own automobile?
4. Do you do your own ironing?

5. Do you clean your own house?
6. Do you paint your own house when it needs repainting?
7. Do you do your own mechanical repairs on your automobile?

I realize that the answer may very well be yes to some, or all of these questions. My guess is that there are two scenarios under which you may have answered yes.

Scenario Number One:

If you are fresh out of medical school and just beginning to earn income, you are probably still doing some of these chores. This is still out of necessity, not necessarily choice. Money is still in short supply and may continue to be for a couple of years. However, as you earn more money, you will begin to relinquish and delegate the above chores one by one.

Scenario Number Two:

The second scenario is that you do the chores, simply because you enjoy them and may even find them relaxing. For example, I employed a lawn service for many years. Here in Texas we mow our lawns twelve months a year. When my children reached their teens, I decided to stop using a lawn service, buy lawn equipment, and teach my children the value of a good work ethic. Well, as I stated before, "the best laid plans . . ." My children decided not to "buy into" the whole "yard mowing" lesson. I can only assume it was not in their business plans, so they delegated it, back to me. Although my kids never really mowed the entire lawn, my son did run over our trampoline once. And I have to admit, running over a trampoline with a push mower is quite a feat in itself.

However, as my wife and I began mowing the lawn with (or mostly without), the children, we both found it to be relaxing. I couldn't hear my cell phone over the mower, and the children didn't dare approach me and ask me for something while I was mowing for fear I'll ask them to help. I have also found that it is very relaxing to sit on the porch with a cold beer and watch someone else mow my lawn.

What about the rest of the list? Well, if you are like me, I struggle to even find the time to delegate my necessary chores to others, much less the time to do them myself. My automotive oil change vendor is next door to a fast food restaurant where I can grab lunch while my oil is changed. These guys can change oil, fluids and filters quicker than the restaurant can serve me a hamburger that was cooked before I even ordered. But it still kills me to have to go and get it done. I'm not sure why. Probably because I know I have to. Do you enjoy taking and picking up your clothes from the dry cleaners? I don't. Did you know you have options for all of the above? Why not ask your nurse, administrative assistant, or any other trusted staff member to help you have your oil changed or take your clothes to the dry cleaners? If you find it relaxing, great, knock yourself out doing it. Otherwise, let it go. You do not get paid to do it, and remember, you cannot do what you do get paid to do while you are away doing mundane chores. Think about what it is *costing* you to do these chores.

If, for whatever reason, you do not have the option to delegate these various items, ask your vendors if they have a service which will come to you. For a promise of steady business, most vendors can become very flexible.

If you do allow one of your employees to occasionally drive your vehicle on errands for you, or even if they drive their own vehicle on your errands, let your personal insurance agent know. The increase in insurance premium, if any, is well worth the additional time you will have once you are freed up from these daily chores. You will find very quickly that the increase in premium correlates to the increase in your quality of life.

I currently have a vendor that comes to my office building to wash my vehicles. My dry cleaner picks up and delivers my clothes. We even have neighborhood children who offer to walk our dog.

If you enjoy doing any of these things, again, I suggest you continue to do them. Like any hobby, doing something you enjoy will relieve stress and ultimately make you a healthier and more productive person. If, on the other hand, you find these tasks annoying or burdensome, have someone else do them for you.

Do not stress about initially setting up these relationships. In most cases you should have a staff person that can do this for you also. If you have no staff or spouse capable of this task, then go ahead and bite the bullet and set these relationships up. Once they are established they can last many years.

Let's now look at similar situations inside your business:

- Do you hire and fire your own staff?
- Do you, or does someone in your office do your own payroll each week?
- Did you set up 401 K for your employees, or did you contract it out?
- Do you do your own billing, collect your own receivables?
- Do you handle your own marketing and advertising?
- Do you handle your own e-mails?
- Do you order your own supplies and equipment?
- Do you handle issues with your landlord or leasing agent?

If you said yes to any of these, you are not alone. If I take this example far enough, it becomes as plain as day.

If I asked you if you answered the phones in your medical practice or scheduled your patients' appointments, chances are you would say no. There are a number of reasons that you do not schedule your own appointments. The main reason is that you were taught in medical school the importance of a good staff. In addition, as long as you can remember, whenever you walked into an office, you were greeted by a receptionist behind a window or desk.

There is a very good chance that your current office is set up, physically, just like the one you went to as a patient, when you were a child. Now be honest, how similar is your office setup today compared to your own pediatrician's? Is it almost identical? Can you imagine where society would be today, if you practiced medicine the same now as it was when you were a child? Can you imagine working and running your business now without the benefit of computers, fax machines, courier services, or e-mail?

Not a pretty picture. What I am trying to present here is that times change. Theoretically, you could have been taught to delegate, to some degree, almost every single task that I have addressed. I have suggested to many a physician to arrive in the morning, attend (not conduct) a 15 minute staff meeting, see patients, attend a 15 minute debriefing with your administrative assistant, and leave the office. Delegate the remainder of your practice to staff.

And had you been taught the above business model in medical school, you would feel much more comfortable with it than you do hearing it from me for the first time. Had you been exposed to these concepts earlier, they would have at least been on your list of things to eventually accomplish. Look around at some of your colleagues. What separates the successful from the ultra successful? Some of your colleagues no longer perform the above functions simply because over time, they have become too successful to have the time to do them.

Obviously they are very talented at what they do. Did they become successful and then talented, or talented and then successful? I realize that the longer you practice your skill the better you become. However, you were obviously talented enough to get through medical school. You have already pushed past, whatever you had to push past, to get to where you are. Otherwise you would not be here today.

Let me ask you a very important question. At what point are you going to maximize your talent to become as successful as you can be? Understand that I am absolutely not talking only about monetary compensation here. As I have previously stated, I am talking about issues ranging from your personal health, spirituality, hobbies, family, as well as professional achievements. If you do what you are good at, and what you have been trained for, and allow other professionals around you do the same, you will be pleasantly surprised at what can happen in all aspects of your life.

Letting go of important responsibilities, both large and small, is a very challenging task. Even letting go may require skills that you do not currently possess. However, don't worry; there is a consultant for virtually every task known to man these days. When you begin to "let go", it is imperative that it be done slowly, and with a great deal of forethought. This is unfortunately, one of those chores that will absolutely require a fair amount of your personal input, at least in the beginning.

Understand that delegating to a person who is not capable of adequately handling your personal business, could be disastrous.

You will not be able to concentrate and focus your energies on your profession if you are constantly wondering if this task or that task has been accomplished. There are simple checks and balances to put in place to ensure adequate performance from everyone in your employment.

Although consultants are very skilled at implementing this change, you will be required to make decisions that will establish the general direction of the change. You will need to decide for yourself, how much control you feel comfortable relinquishing. A good way to initiate this change is to take a several step approach. Step one, visualize what you feel is realistically achievable. If your office currently consists of you and one receptionist, it may be naïve to think that you could delegate more to her than she is currently handling.

Aside from a time constraint, with a one person office consisting of a person hired to be a receptionist, you could easily run into a knowledge problem. If you have not read "The Peter Principle", by Dr. Laurence Peter and Raymond Hull, you should order it and read it. It's dated, but so are most of us. However, this is the perfect time to point out that had you had the above business model in mind before you hired your second staff member, you may already be in a much better position to proceed. But, employee turnover is quite possibly another area of concern for your office, so maybe we can address two things at once.

"Flattery will get you everywhere"

After you visualize how you would like your office to function, it's time to move to step two. Step two is to find an office that is functioning smoothly, and imitate what they are doing. If you can't think of another physician's office to visit, pick up the phone and call some of your friends that are physicians. It will not take you long to find what you are looking for. Once you identify another office you would like to visit, don't be afraid to pick up the phone and call that physician. Some of the more successful physicians will also share with you their detailed exit strategy. When the time comes for them to retire, they already know who will purchase their practice. People love to talk about their success stories, and are more than willing to give you advice. Asking a successful physician to share his business secrets with you is like asking a mother to share with you all the many ways that their child is special. Most of us would go on forever.

Once you arrive onsite, and after initial introductions, be up front with your host. I strongly suggest that the first statement you make is to ensure your host that you will only spend a specific amount of time visiting, and I recommend you honor that commitment. You will need to ask him for follow up advice later down the road, and if he cannot trust you will be respectful of his time, you will find it difficult to reach him again after your initial visit. For example, you probably have patients that you will speak with on the phone because you know they are "quick and to the point" and other patients that you probably have to delegate to staff because you know that are going to be long-winded. Tell your host you have heard that the manner in which he operates his office is impressive. At times, this is, unfortunately, where egos can come into play. To acknowledge that someone has done it better than you is more than some professionals can handle. This, however, does not have to be the end of the line for improvement. Most consultants have the necessary skills to facilitate, or altogether avoid, this situation. Consultants can readily take you into offices that are operated much more efficiently than yours, without you having to get involved in the initial process.

"Keep everything in perspective"

A consultant can also take you into offices that are operated much worse than yours; there is almost always someone on both ends of the spectrum. When you visit another facility, just be yourself. Honest, sincere flattery, especially in the business world, is not offensive, or threatening. So if you are impressed, be sure and tell your hosting physician. Explain that you would like to set your office up in a similar manner and would like to visit their facility again in the future. As the old saying goes, imitation is the best form of flattery.

Again, most successful professionals are like proud parents. They realize they have produced something enviable and are usually more than willing to show off their accomplishments. In some competitive situations, the more distance between you and the physician you want to tour, the better.

"Just get up and get away"

Let me share from personal experience. When choosing a successful clinic to visit, I will actually identify a city I want to visit first, and then find a physician in that city. This allows me a justified day off, with travel to a city that I intentionally picked out. This can also be advantageous from a tax standpoint, but address that issue with your CPA as I do not give tax advice. Touring a facility in another town offers some additional advantages. If you are out of town, that generally means you have coverage for your clinic, so your mind is on what you are touring, not what is going on at the office. Secondly, the further you are from your home market, the more comfortable the hosting physician will feel. As you tour, remember this is a sample of what you can do. You are not bound by anything this particular facility does. This just represents what is possible. It is similar to a cafeteria line. If you see something you like, take it. If you see something you don't like, pass it up.

I have, in some industries, found people so successful that I almost always use them as the touring model, regardless of the distance my client must travel. This also keeps the host professional, in a mode of wanting to continue to improve so I can always see new processes.

It is possible to cross industry lines when trying to model another successful company. However, this can be a bit more challenging. Few could argue that McDonalds is a modern day success, even if you don't like their hamburgers. But when I take a physician into a McDonald's restaurant and try to explain the processes, and the reasoning behind them, sometimes it can be a struggle.

"You will find what you search for"

As I stated earlier, finding successful models is not as difficult as you might imagine. Remember some of the more difficult situations you had to diagnose when you were just starting out? How much easier are they for you to spot now? Chances are things haven't changed. You've just gotten better at identifying these challenges. This is no different than cultivating the ability to identify successful businesses.

Step three, takes only a little time. This is where you ask yourself how much of this is possible, and in what time frame. Again, you must first be honest with yourself. You may need some unbiased opinions at this stage of the game. You need to balance your new goals with your current individual situation. You may be able to run your implementation plans past the person whose facility you toured. You could also use a mentor or a consultant. I do not, however, recommend asking for your staff's input too early in the process, for several reasons. Employees, like most people, do not like change. Additionally, staff may have a tendency to push back on issues that increase, or even decrease their individual work loads. And most importantly, you did not hire them to be "change agents", and most of them will not have the knowledge or skill set necessary to do it successfully.

"Baby steps"

Try to be open-minded and objective about this entire process, and do not become defensive, impatient or frustrated. I realize this can be difficult, but it is a necessary step for improvement. Successful people can sense frustration, defensiveness and insincerity. The input you will need to be successful may cease if people sense any insincerity on your part.

The initial data you receive may be overwhelming. Much of how you process this initial data will be influenced by your most basic business philosophy. Even if it is not in writing, (and it should be), be sure you are clear on what your business philosophy is. If you are trying to implement something in your organization that goes against your most basic beliefs, you will ultimately fail. For instance, if the physician that you are trying to model believes in empowering employees, and you believe that employees need close and strict supervision, you will not, in all likelihood, be able to make that transition. This is not to say that you cannot succeed with your philosophy. It does mean that you should choose a different physician after whom to model your business.

"Don't do as I do, do as I say"

I once worked with a banker who insisted on signing every single check that was issued by that bank. I was in his office one day when an executive vice president brought in a phone bill that needed to be paid. The bill was around $350.00 dollars. The bank had three branches and over thirty employees, with three executive Vice Presidents on site. If you feel the need for this much control, your options may be limited in some areas.

"Measure twice, cut once"

Just remember that there is no area of responsibility inside an office environment that cannot be reduced to writing, hence creating a process. Once the process is in place, you simply have to implement it. If you have a recurring problem, it will most likely be the person responsible for the process, as opposed to the process itself. You should not continually change a process to match the strengths and weaknesses of an employee. Instead, you should take additional time to hire someone with adequate skills to perform the required, previously established processes. A process is designed to accomplish a goal. It was created and established for that purpose alone, with no particular person in mind. If a process is created properly, it can be measured. Furthermore, all processes should be assigned to a specific staff member, otherwise the process will not typically be very useful. Generally speaking, if a process belongs to everyone, it belongs to no one. Ultimately, in management you need to know a very important principal and that is, "If you cannot measure it, you cannot manage it".

This is true for virtually every aspect of management. Do not set yourself and your employees up for failure. Be sure that every responsibility can be measured. What is important to remember here is that "good can be the enemy of the best". You should do what you do best, and what you most enjoy doing. Do what you know and love, and allow others to do the same. Peace of mind will surely follow.

CHAPTER 3

What do you keep, and what do you lose?

"There are costs and risks to a program of action,
but they are far less than the long-range risks and costs
of comfortable inaction" ~John F. Kennedy.

Say a pound of coal on the open market is worth $1.50, turn that coal into a one carat diamond and it is worth $2,000. There are two basic questions that I use when addressing the issue of which responsibilities to keep and which responsibilities to delegate. The answers to these questions will guide you in a general direction on making these decisions. The first question is, "Do you have to have a specific skill set to perform the particular task in question?" If the answer is yes, then you should strongly consider keeping that task for yourself. If, on the other hand, the answer is no, then perhaps you might consider delegating that task to a staff person.

"Show me the money"

The second question is, "Who is handling my money?" This is obviously a big question. I can tell you that I have had money, and I have not had money, and I much prefer to have money. The knowledge and skills you learned in medical school are valuable in the market place, and that is also how you make your living. The value or worth is not actually created until you apply those learned skills on a patient. By that I mean that nothing really happens until you begin actively working on a patient. However, once you begin patient treatment, the business side, otherwise known as overhead, of your profession is born. Everything in your clinic can be categorized as either an asset or a liability. The truth is other than your original treatment of the patient, most everything else in your practice is overhead. You cannot eliminate overhead, you can only manage it. Your best plan of action is to acknowledge the business side of your practice as a factual event, and simply get proficient at dealing with it.

You must make a profit to keep the doors open. However, keeping the doors open is just the beginning. Not a single professional whom I have ever interviewed has ever told me that they chose their careers so they could operate a facility and make just enough money to keep the doors open.

"There is no business like show business"

The business side of medicine is ugly. Society would, in general, prefer to just ignore it, act as if it doesn't exist at all. You know, the Ostrich Theory. And it is easy to understand why. For one person to make money because another person is ill, just seems wrong. But it is not wrong because that is not what medicine is. Medicine is when one individual heals another person, and truth be told, it is probably the most honorable professions there is. I acknowledge that most physicians have extremely high I.Q.'s, and are challenged by the scientific aspects of medicine. Almost all physicians were drawn to medicine because of a desire to help people, not because it pays well. Most physicians are practicing medicine to help cure illness "one patient at a time". In fact, this very book is written because physicians are just now having to learn how to be businessmen and businesswomen, as well as physicians.

There are as many reasons why we choose the profession we choose. Whatever your reasons, to maintain a medical practice you must make a profit. In its most simple definition, profit is simply what is left over after everyone and everything else is paid. The trap to watch out for here is the phrase "everyone and everything."

You must decide how to keep a handle on your expenses, and who will actually do it. The most important thing to remember is that there are ratios for almost everything you are trying to monitor. There are statistics on everything from how much you should be paying for office supplies and equipment, to how to compensate employees. In each category you should establish parameters or ratios, or even a monthly budget, and then spend a very brief time reviewing these categories at the end of the month to ensure compliance.

Under this scenario, you do not need to purchase office supplies, equipment, or do payroll yourself, you just need processes in place to ensure they are all being handled properly.

"Need to know"

The military has a term that I adopted when I was elected Mayor, called "need to know". All that means is that you are told what you "need to know", and there are many issues you simply don't need to know. One of the most sensitive issues you will encounter in your practice is payroll. In small offices this can be a tremendously disruptive issue. As soon as one of your staff members discovers what another staff member is earning, the wheels of prosperity can quickly grind to a halt. On the flip side, without the flexibility to pay each person what he or she is actually worth, in regards to the value they bring to your practice, you will be unable to attract the best team members possible. I strongly suggest using a payroll service to handle this function.

Most good payroll companies can also handle your 401K plans and your health insurance on a pre-tax basis. One of the most practical features a payroll service offers is a service called "run as is." This feature will allow you to set your payroll up on a weekly, bi-monthly or monthly basis, then allow it to run automatically without further input from you. In the event you are traveling, or just out of the office when it comes time to call in payroll, the payroll service can be instructed to just run the payroll as it was originally set up based on a 40 hour week. You can then reconcile the differences with your employees after you return. No matter how you handle your expenses, just remember that no one, and I truly mean no one, will handle your money quite as prudently as you will.

Another area, and probably the largest, where money tends to slip away is your account receivables. Make no mistake about one very simple fact—the money on that accounts receivable report belongs to you. You've already paid the rent, the employees, the government, the insurance, and no telling who else, so the remainder is yours, theoretically. But if your money remains "on the books", then even though it is yours, it is not doing you any good. Regardless of where you are in life, financially speaking, ask yourself a very basic question, "How would my current financial situation change today if the amount of money owed to me on my accounts receivables, was sitting in my bank account instead of on my books?" Even at current short term CD rates, the interest that you are losing on that money starts to add up quickly. Did you know that there are companies, and providers, that have unwritten policies to not pay any bill until someone calls to inquire about payment, and to verify that all information is correct? As incredible-as that sounds, think about the money an insurance carrier would make, on interest alone, with that policy in place. It is not uncommon for the incorrect amount to be paid on claims as well. If your staff does not call to question the incorrect payment, you have just lost money.

Mistakes on reimbursements are common in the medical and insurance industry. Insurance providers actually receive interest on overnight deposits. I have seen that interest number as high as 9% on these deposits. So the longer the insurance company holds your payments, and hundreds of other clinics just like yours, the more money these companies have in the bank drawing interest.

Can you imagine the money these companies are making simply by delaying payment of claims by even a day or two, not to mention a month or more? Do you have someone on your payroll to collect money? If so, what formulas do you use to establish his or her effectiveness? If you do not have anyone on your staff dedicated to collect money, I would recommend you revisit that decision. It may prove to be the wisest move you make.

Have you ever thought about trying to operate your practice without the benefit of a receptionist or a nurse? Probably not. It would be difficult to function without someone to greet your patients, bill your clients and follow up with your vendors.

So why, when you have successfully performed everything that is required to operate a profitable practice, would you not aggressively pursue what is rightfully yours—your fees? If all your customers sent in checks tomorrow, how many days would you be willing to leave them sitting in envelopes in your desk drawer, simply because you didn't have enough staff to fill out a deposit slip and drive to the bank? If that number is longer than one business day, it must be great to be you.

Regardless of what type of practice you operate, you should have firsthand knowledge on how much of your money is in the 30 day, 60 day, 90 day, and over 90 day column. There are established percentages on the probability of collecting monies within each column. Can you guess which one will be the most difficult to collect?

If you cannot take any other action on this issue, at least have your staff start the collecting process from the Z's and work backwards. The Z's have probably never been called and you may realize a bit of a spike in your cash flow for even this minimal effort. Needless to say, there are many other methods to improve accounts receivables collections. And when you improve collections, you improve cash flow, and that, my friend, is literally money in the bank.

CHAPTER 4

Marketing Your Practice

*"Marketing is not the art of finding clever ways
to dispose of what you make. It is the art of creating
genuine customer value." ~ Philip Kotler*

Have you ever been practicing your trade, when you found yourself thinking "I really am good at what I do"? Well, have you ever had that thought while having a staff meeting, designing patient literature, or talking to your receptionist about how you would like the phones to be answered? Probably not. Would you believe that there are people who do enjoy staff meetings, advertising and expense ratios? I know because I am one of them.

All of the above are examples of marketing. Some professionals are so bad at marketing, they decide it is not necessary and don't do it at all. Others are smart enough to realize its importance, so they implement a policy or even hire someone, so they feel better about this area of the business. Many people do this knowing they are not actually accomplishing anything, but they feel it is at least a step in the right direction. And it actually may be. Would you invest in a piece of diagnostic medical equipment that may or may not be working? How comfortable would you feel writing a check to your X-Ray vendor if you discovered that the machine only worked part of the time, and when it malfunctioned, it was programmed to automatically show the healthy profile of whatever gender you were x-raying? I am going to guess you probably would not be willing to pay good money for a product or service that only worked some of the time.

Marketing is a science, not an art. Many aspects can be measured quantitatively. And the areas that need to be measured qualitatively are not that difficult to assess. Before we discuss marketing, let us decide whether you need to do it or not. If you do, read on. If you don't think you do, you may want to skip this chapter.

If you are preparing to retire and have already found a buyer for your practice, then you are probably past needing to market. If you have more business than you can handle, from a source that will remain consistent, and there are many businesses that do, then you just need to manage the growth and profitability opportunities that you have already created. If you are not one of those two types of (fortunate) practices, in my opinion, you need to market.

Marketing, sales and advertising, are all very similar when you are discussing a small business. The differences do not become apparent until you start applying the principals at much larger organizations, usually with annual income over three million. For the sake of brevity, I am only going to address the needs of smaller practices.

As you might imagine, there are infinite methods to market your practice. Marketing can include hiring a person to do nothing but make sales calls, design web pages, handle direct mail, telemarketing, publish in trade journals, and network, just to touch on a few. Entire books have been written on virtually each of these, as well as other types of marketing approaches. *The marketing approach that is best suited to your practice will be tied specifically back to your business goals and your overall direction.* All marketing can be outsourced. Just think of the advantages of paying for something only when you are using it, or better yet, only when it is successful.

Everything you do after you open your practice is marketing, especially if you live in the same community you work in. All marketing, like politics, is local. You can sponsor youth sporting teams. I know a man in my community who waits until all the sponsorships are final, and then offers to sponsor every remaining team that was unable to secure a sponsor. I have seen him sponsor as many as 30 Little League baseball teams, at a cost of $150 each, in one summer season. Now that is making a statement about community involvement. The good news is that you do not have to spend that kind of cash to make an impact. The local youth teams are appreciative of anything they can get. If you want to make an even larger statement, then you can coach a youth sports team. If you make this commitment, be prepared to see it through to the end. And make especially sure you have the skills required to deal with children several days a week.

You can get involved with local governments such as City Councils, School Boards or PTA's. All of these types of community involvement will allow you to interact with local people. From these acquaintances, new friendships are formed and new networking opportunities evolve. Each of these options invites more responsibilities, so make sure you have the time and resources available before you commit. You want to be perceived as a reputable person who above all else, can be counted on.

As you look to new areas to market, consider the local industry. Depending on what type of clinic you operate, this may be an excellent source of business. You can have your staff approach any industry, even small businesses with only a few employees, to become their company physician. If this is not feasible, you can offer to consult on a fee basis just to ensure companies are getting accurate information from their current provider. Any person you meet can eventually become a client or customer of yours.

As you can see, marketing opportunities are endless. Who would have ever thought that one day you would see the Nike "swoosh" on virtually every professional and college football team jersey. Marketing a medical practice is as much a business as actually providing the medical services. The big question is, "Do you possess the same level of skill to market your practice as you do to practice medicine?" If not, outsource it.

If you think that doing nothing is a safe bet, you are wrong. Believe me when I tell you that doing nothing gets noticed just as much as doing something. This is mainly because while you are doing nothing, the community around you is continuing to remain active. There are still Rotary Clubs, Lions Clubs, Businessman's Prayer Groups, Industry Associations, and every other type of meeting you can possibly imagine, still happening everyday in your community. For example, if just one healthcare professional is attending those meetings, eventually the question will come up, "I wonder why Dr. So and So never attends any of these meetings?" If you are a physician, you will still be in luck here because in many cases there are no other physicians attending these meetings, short of a local Rotary Club. Think of the possibilities of being the only one in each of these groups. Eventually these clubs will ask your opinion on every medical question that arises. You will be the expert in the community on anything to do with health related issues.

Each of the above mentioned clubs is important and can have a positive impact on your career. However, the most important clubs, as I stated before, are often the ones associated with various specific industries. Many organizations appreciate having involvement from local business people as part of their membership. This type of association can often lead to opportunities to be the keynote speaker at these meetings.

Speaking at different functions, however small, will open a wide variety of offers and opportunities. The topics you agree to speak on should always be chosen by you, so it will always be an area you feel comfortable with. This is one of the most effective areas of marketing in today's business environment, and the most overlooked.

Aside from having something interesting to say, you also have to be comfortable with your ability to speak in public. If you have these skills, you probably already know it. If you are not sure whether or not you have that skill, then you may need to check with someone close to you who will be honest with you. This is not to say you do not have public speaking skills, but you may want a second opinion before you book a talk before a group of other professionals whom you live and work with.

If you decide that you need to hone your public speaking skills, there are several ways to accomplish this. You can look on the internet or in the local phonebook for Toastmasters. This is a great group of people that meet on a regular basis to work on their public speaking skills. As a physician, once you are comfortable with public speaking, you will have endless opportunities to speak, as the public always wants to hear about the latest in healthcare.

Have you ever thought about donating your services for free at your local school district? You can offer to contribute your services, when and if necessary, to any of the local schools in your community. This can include anything from helping out with flu shots to attending the high school football games for support. For instance, there was an issue recently in Texas related to a meningitis outbreak. There are a number of ways a local physician could have become involved in this issue. These opportunities can range from preparing a fact sheet on the bacteria to be distributed to the children to take home to their parents, giving talks at the PTA meetings, to talking at an entire school assembly. This is, of course, just one example. What affects *your* community and business will be different. That's not what is important. What is important is your frame of mind. Learn to check the local news issue regarding current issues and figure out how to insert yourself and your business in that picture. You then immediately become the local expert.

Have you ever been listening to a news report about a breaking news story, and heard the broadcaster switch to an interview of a person speaking on that specific issue as an authority figure? Have you ever wondered who the speakers are, and where the news station found them? In many cases these people being interviewed simply called the station to give their opinion of the situation. There may have been fifty people calling the station with an opinion on that subject. But if one of those people presents themselves as an expert on the present topic, who do you think they will put on the radio? Once you are put on the radio addressing any particular issue, you are perceived an expert on that issue.

When it comes to marketing, whichever type you choose, be consistent. No marketing produces overnight results. I strongly suggest that you consult with someone to assist you in making these basic decisions, as well as someone to assist you in creating any printed materials. Think back about the marketing materials that cross your desk, whether they are medical related or not, and decide what you like about them. Always try to mimic success. However, keep in mind that you are not, in most cases, marketing to others in the same line of business. Make sure you are clear on who you are marketing to. Once you identify who your target market is, it is best to speak with experts in that industry. Don't be afraid to ask "dumb" questions. If you are saying to yourself right now, "I don't have that kind of time available", then again, this is an important area, and it should be outsourced.

There are a tremendous number of essential tasks associated with the business side of your practice, but they have absolutely nothing do to with the practice of medicine. Try, on a daily basis, to do first what you are good at, and what you enjoy doing. Then delegate all the remaining tasks that are essential, but which you have no interest in doing. This particular process can become overwhelming if you let it. Just set reasonable goals, and expect everyone in your organization, including yourself, to just make measurable progress in reasonable time. One day you will look back and be very satisfied that you made the decision to work "on your business, not in your business". Crossing your fingers and hoping that these processes happen is a very poor business plan. Trust me when I tell you that when I was younger I tried the cross-fingered approach, and it didn't work out too well for me.

CHAPTER 5

Where Can You Partner?

"In the past a leader was a boss. Today's leaders must be partners with their people, they no longer can lead solely based on positional power" ~ Ken Blanchard

Where and who can you partner with in today's business and medical environment? The better question here is where can't you partner? Have you ever seen a McDonald's restaurant located inside an Exxon gas station? Have you seen a Subway sandwich shop inside a Chevron gas station? If this question seems redundant, it is. How often do you find yourself thinking about a better way to do what you specialize in? It is a simple, natural question to ask, "How can I perform my job more efficiently and more effectively?

There are a number of reasons to partner with various other companies. The reasons include, but are not limited to, reducing transaction cost on a per transaction basis, associating with a company that creates more selling opportunities, and as a result of that, establishing a secure income stream, and countless others. In the medical industry, many of these agreements have been affected by legislation called the Stark Laws. The legislation was created because politicians became uncomfortable with some existing partnering agreements. In reality, partnering arrangements have been in existence in all industries for a long, long time. Make sure and run any new, or existing, partnering agreements you have through your attorney. It is always better to be safe than sorry. As long as the agreements are legal, ethical and moral, they can actually improve patient care.

A physician needs to constantly reevaluate which necessary services should be outsourced, and when it is time to bring the service in-house. Services such as x-rays and physical therapy are among a few services that can be brought in-house, if you have the volume to justify the expense.

There are many new and exciting partnering and cost sharing arrangements between physicians and other medical services providers.

Aside from the original examples I stated above with the x-ray and physical therapy, there are many other examples. It does, however, depend in some degree, on what your specialty is. With that in mind, look below at some of the possible pairings:

a) Chiropractors and Occupational medical care physicians
b) Occupational care physicians and Orthopedic surgeons
c) Orthopedic Surgeons and Physical Therapy Clinics
d) Internalists and Pain management physicians
e) Orthopedic surgeons and splint companies

Aside from these obvious associations, there are many physician and non medical profession partnerships available to consider. Some of the successful ones I've seen include:

a) Physicians and professional sports teams
b) Physicians and radio talk stations
c) Physicians and local schools
d) Physicians and attorneys
e) Physicians and insurance companies
f) Physicians and pharmaceutical representatives

Many of the above partnerships are compensated positions. That does not make them any less of a partnership. The basic premise that needs to be met is that the arrangement is mutually beneficial to all parties involved. This area of partnering is one of the most exciting opportunities in today's business environment. The opportunities that are available in today's market place are limited only by your imagination. As I stated in the beginning, who would have ever thought that Nike would partner with almost every sporting team in the world? Or at least it seems like it.

There are many opportunities available to you that you are already aware of, but you simply do not have the time and energy to pursue them. If you think they would be beneficial, but have no time to establish them, outsource it to a consultant. To create other opportunities you simply have to invest some time thinking about who benefits from your services, upstream and downstream. By upstream I am referring to where your patients originate from. And by downstream I simply am referring to where your patients need to be referred to when they leave your office. You need to learn to think of your practice and your patients on a global scale.

When you see a patient, you are originally focused on diagnosing and curing that patient, as well you should be. But have you ever stopped to think about the number of additional, non-medical activities that office visit includes? They are endless. And once the patient shows up at your practice, imagine the number of additional events that could be triggered by that visit. There are obviously all the medical issues, such as x-rays, splints, therapy, and possible additional diagnostic tests, among the many other medical aspects of a patient visit that may be necessary. But there are additional aspects such as billing, insurance, collections, patient follow up, all of which contain possible partnering relationships. The partnership may help you treat your patients more efficiently and effectively. Or it may help you address the administrative aspect of your practice such as billing, collecting and patient follow up. If it improves patient care, it should be seriously considered.

CHAPTER 6

Looking Ahead

"Doing the same thing over and over, and expecting different results is Webster's definition of insanity."

Regardless of where you are in life, you probably will not be there for long. Life simply changes too quickly. So the issue remains: ten years from now, you will arrive, but the question is, where? Give it some thought while you have ample time to affect directional changes that will keep you on track to where you want to be.

Several years ago, a preacher friend of mine and I were discussing a possible joint business venture together. While researching all the wide array of possible ventures available, we took an inventory of our skills. We both had sufficient people skills. His strength was oratory and mine was my business background. Neither of us wanted to change careers, we just wanted a new challenge, and possibly some additional income. In discussing our options, he asked me where I wanted this sideline business to take us. My answer was a simple summation of my hobbies. I stated that I love to play golf and I love to travel. I further realized that when I travel, I prefer to stay in locations that have golf available. Since we had both already worked as consultants, the answer was obvious. Why not add resort hotel properties to our list of consulting clients? I would then be able to stay at resorts, play golf and continue to do what I am best at: consulting.

It is just about that easy. Even if you love everything about your current life, you must be prepared to take action to maintain that life. Just ask your self some simple questions. In ten years, where do I want to be and what do I want to be doing? With your current lifestyle pace, what type of health will you be in? If you have children, how old will they be? What activities will they be involved in? Your answer could range from wanting to coach their little league baseball team to being able to visit them regularly at college. As you already realize, there are no right or wrong answers. After you have asked yourself these questions, then you only need to decide if your current activities and decisions are going to put you in a position to accomplish all the things you have already listed.

It is so important for me to emphasize here that there is no right or wrong dream, assuming of course, that your choices are healthy and legal. I have always believed that a balanced life is a fruitful life. However, if you work seven days a week now and want to continue to work seven days a week, that's your decision. Just be sure to acknowledge the consequences. When I was younger and my children were all in diapers, I found myself working ten to twelve hours a day. I didn't realize it at the time, but I was doing it for two reasons. First, I was trying to build a business. And second, building a business was easier than raising three children in diapers. I did it completely unconsciously at the time. Now that I am older, and my children are going off to college, my goals are different. I still love to work, and do not see myself ever retiring. However, I prefer to work less than when I was younger. It does not always work out that way, but I do my best to plan my week in advance as much as possible. This gives me more time to spend with my family and to write.

Knowing what I want, gives me more options when making daily decisions. It is so interesting to me to watch myself as my interests change. Only when I look back over several decisions I have made, do I realize that my interests, and therefore my priorities, are changing. Change is inevitable. Intelligent people realize it is best to manage change just like you mange finances, health, relationships or any other aspect of your life.

As soon as I realize my interests are changing, I schedule some down time to analyze this change. I need to know what I am adding to my life and what I am giving up. Is my new interest consistent with my other hobbies? I believe that there are two basic reasons why people do not ask themselves these questions. First, I believe that many people are just not aware of the obvious. So they plod along day after day, taking only what life gives. They believe they have no control over their destinies. How sad is that?

The second reason is a little more complex. I believe that many people do originally ask themselves these questions. Or they are at the very least conscious of this type of "self-assessments". This is where it gets complicated; they do not like the answers, so they ignore the entire process. This happens, in many cases, when the questions raise obvious conflicts in life. For instance, you tell yourself that you want to build your business, and make a name for yourself as the best in the area of your specialty. On the other hand, you tell yourself that you will be the best spouse and parent ever. You want to be much better than your own parents, who you probably thought made a couple of mistakes along the way.

Both are noble goals, but they conflict with each other. I believe a person can accomplish almost anything they set their mind to. However, you must make choices. You've heard it said a million times before, virtually no one on their death beds wishes they had spent more time at work. I believe activity and accomplishment is what life is all about. Rest and relaxation should be a necessity, not an objective. It is time to refocus your energies on your practice of medicine. Be smart enough to do what you do best, and delegate the rest.

Think back right now on the three most exciting times in your life. I'd be willing to bet most all of your best memories started with a simple plan of action.

At the time of publishing, Jerry Shults owned The Chronic Pain Institute and Inner Loop Physical Therapy, both healthcare facilities located in Houston, Texas. Jerry also consults in the medical industry and can be reached at (281) 481-4357. His website is *www.jerryshults.com* and he can be reached via email at *theauthor@jerryshults.com*.